Celebrations!

Hanukkah

Mandy Ross

Heinemann
LIBRARY

H www.heinemann.co.uk/library
Visit our website to find out more information about Heinemann Library books.

To order:
☎ Phone 44 (0) 1865 888066
📄 Send a fax to 44 (0) 1865 314091
💻 Visit the Heinemann Bookshop at www.heinemann.co.uk/library to browse our catalogue and order online.

First published in Great Britain by Heinemann Library,
Halley Court, Jordan Hill, Oxford OX2 8EJ
a division of Reed Educational and Professional Publishing Ltd.
Heinemann is a registered trademark of Reed Educational & Professional Publishing Ltd.

OXFORD MELBOURNE AUCKLAND
JOHANNESBURG BLANTYRE GABORONE
IBADAN PORTSMOUTH (NH) USA CHICAGO

Designed by Celia Floyd
Originated by Ambassador Litho Ltd
Printed by Wing King Tong in Hong Kong

ISBN 0 431 13794 3 (hardback)   ISBN 0 431 13802 8 (paperback)
06 05 04 03 02   06 05 04 03 02
10 9 8 7 6 5 4 3 2   10 9 8 7 6 5 4 3 2 1

British Library Cataloguing in Publication Data

Ross, Mandy
  Hanukkah. – (Celebrations)
  1. Hanukkah – Juvenile literature
  I. Title
  394.2'67

Acknowledgements
The Publishers would like to thank the following for permission to reproduce photographs:
AKG Photo, Berlin: S Domingie p15; AKG Photo, London: p21, Erich Lessing p14; Ancient Art & Architecture Collection: p7; Andes Press Agency: Carlos Reyes-Manzo pp5, 12; Bridgeman Art Library: British Library p9; Holy Land Photo Library: Hanan Isachar p20; Mark Azavedo: p16; Powerstock Zefa: p19; Robert Harding Picture Library: E Simanor p8; Stock Market: p10, p11; Trip: H Rogers p4

Cover photograph reproduced with permission of Hutchinson Library

Our thanks to the Bradford Interfaith Education Centre for their comments in the preparation of this book.

Every effort has been made to contact copyright holders of any material reproduced in this book. Any omissions will be rectified in subsequent printings if notice is given to the Publisher.

Contents

Words printed in **bold letters like these** are explained in the glossary.

Hanukkah

In the dark days of winter, Jewish people all around the world celebrate Hanukkah, the festival of lights. Every evening for eight days they light candles to remember a **miracle** long ago, and how they won their freedom.

Hanukkah is a happy time. Children give and receive presents, and there is special food to eat, songs to sing and games to play. Families gather together for celebrations at home.

This young girl is celebrating Hanukkah. She is lighting the candles in the **hanukiah**. The ninth candle, in the middle, is used to light the others.

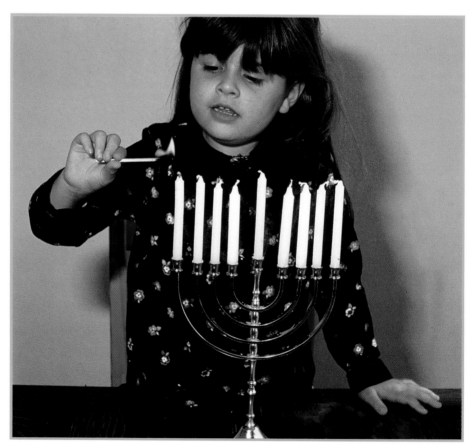

What is Judaism?

Judaism is an ancient **religion**. Jewish people pray to one God, just as they did 4000 years ago. They go to the **synagogue** to pray and to read from their **holy** book, the **Hebrew Bible**. The Torah scrolls contain part of the Bible.

A **rabbi** leading prayers in the synagogue. The light above her is called the **ner tamid**. It is a symbol of God's presence.

The story of Hanukkah

Over 2000 years ago, in the second century **BCE**, the Syrians ruled Judea, where many Jews lived. The Jews believed in one God and **worshipped** at their magnificent **temple** in Jerusalem. The Syrians worshipped other gods, but they let the Jews follow their own **religion**.

But then a Syrian king called Antiochus came to power. He was a cruel king, and he wanted to force everyone to follow his religion, worshipping many gods.

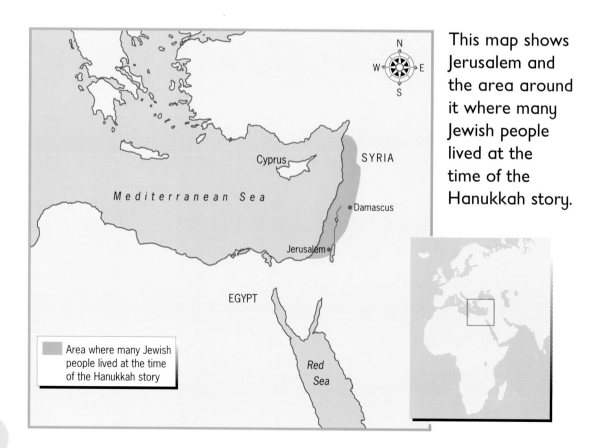

This map shows Jerusalem and the area around it where many Jewish people lived at the time of the Hanukkah story.

Area where many Jewish people lived at the time of the Hanukkah story

The Jews were no longer allowed to worship God in their temple. King Antiochus ordered soldiers to put **idols**, or statues of his gods, in their temple. He told them to make the temple dirty and unfit for worship. The soldiers put out the **ner tamid**, the ever-burning oil lamp. Many Jews were in despair.

But in Modi'in, a town near Jerusalem, there lived an old Jewish priest called Mattathias. He refused to follow King Antiochus' orders. Many Jews took courage from Mattathias, and followed him.

An engraving showing Mattathias leading the Jews in their fight for freedom.

War and a miracle

King Antiochus was furious. He planned a huge battle to crush the Jews once and for all. But Mattathias's son, Judah Maccabee, led a tiny Jewish force against the huge Syrian army. By skill and cunning, the Jewish fighters managed to defeat the Syrians.

The Jews flocked to the **temple** to thank God for their victory. But to their horror, they found that the temple was unclean. They set to work cleaning up and removing the **idols**.

This model shows how the Jews' temple may have looked. The temple was destroyed by the Romans in 70 **CE**.

8

Then they looked for oil to light the **ner tamid**, the ever-burning lamp. But there was only enough oil to burn for one day – and the journey to fetch fresh oil would take eight days.

It was then that Jews believe God sent a **miracle**. One day's oil burned through that day, and the next, and the next. It lasted for eight whole days, until more oil could be fetched. That is why the festival of Hanukkah lasts for eight days.

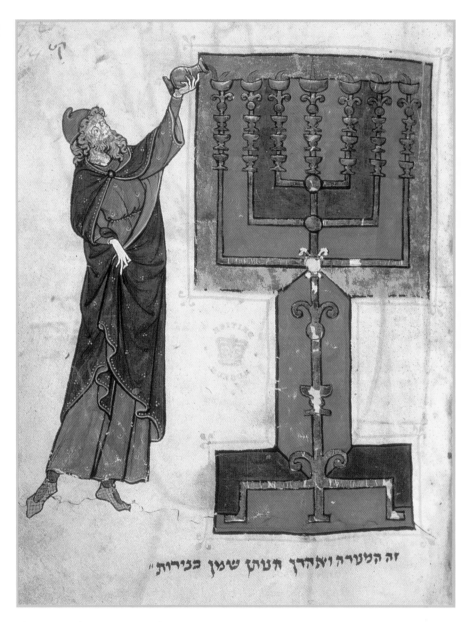

זה המנרה ואהרן נתן שמן בנרות"

Aaron the priest, the brother of Moses, pouring oil to burn in a seven-branched menorah.

Lighting the candles

At home each evening of Hanukkah, Jews light candles in a **hanukiah**. One candle is lit on the first evening, two on the second and so on for the eight days of the festival. The ninth candle is called the 'servant candle'. It is used to light the other candles.

Everyone in the family – even very young children – may take a turn lighting the candles. In some families, each person has their own hanukiah, and then the candlelight is very bright.

This boy is lighting candles in a hanukiah shaped like branches of a tree.

As the candles are lit, this blessing is said or sung in **Hebrew**:

We praise you, Eternal God, ruler of the universe; You sanctify us by Your commandments, and command us to kindle the Hanukkah lights.

בָּרוּךְ אַתָּה יְיָ, אֱלֹהֵינוּ מֶלֶךְ הָעוֹלָם, אֲשֶׁר קִדְּשָׁנוּ בְּמִצְוֹתָיו וְצִוָּנוּ לְהַדְלִיק נֵר שֶׁל חֲנֻכָּה.

The hanukiah is often placed in a window so that people walking past can see it and know about Hanukkah. The candlelight is a symbol and a reminder of God's miracles.

Hanukiot are made in many beautiful different styles, and out of all sorts of materials. Some are designed to burn oil, rather than candles.

Let's celebrate!

Hanukkah is a great time for children! Families and friends get together to share a meal, sing songs, tell stories, play games and give presents. It is traditional to give Hanukkah gelt, or money – or sometimes chocolate money instead.

Lighting the hanukiah in synagogue.

Celebrating Hanukkah at the synagogue

At the **synagogue**, special prayers are said at Hanukkah. Candles are lit in the **hanukiah** as part of the evening services. Many synagogues hold a Hanukkah party, where children and adults can celebrate together.

A traditional Hanukkah song: Ma'oz tsur

Jewish people have sung this Hanukkah song in **Hebrew** for over 500 years. The translation is shown below.

Translation: God, Rock of my salvation, to You our praise is due. Let Your house become a house of prayer and thanksgiving for all peoples. When by Your will all bloodshed ends and enemies cease to scream hate; Then we shall celebrate with joyful song the true dedication of your altar.

Women and Hanukkah

It is traditional for Jewish women to light the candles to celebrate Hanukkah, **Shabbat** and other festivals. Here are some stories about women which are often told at Hanukkah.

Hannah

King Antiochus was trying to force the Jews to leave their **religion**. Hannah was a Jewish widow with seven sons. She encouraged them to stay true to their beliefs. One by one, King Antiochus had the sons killed, until only the youngest was left.

King Antiochus hoped that Hannah would persuade her son to change his mind. But bravely she told him to stay true to his beliefs, and they both died for their religion.

Hannah is remembered for her courage.

Judith

The Syrian army had surrounded a Jewish city. The Syrian general, Holofernes, fell in love with a beautiful young Jewish widow called Judith. Judith cooked him a meal with salty cheese to make him thirsty. Holofernes drank so much wine that he fell into a deep sleep.

Judith's actions helped the Jewish army defeat the Syrians.

While he was asleep, Judith cut off his head. The Jewish army easily defeated the Syrians without their general.

At Hanukkah Jewish people often eat dishes cooked with cheese to remember Judith's story.

Food at Hanukkah

At Hanukkah, Jewish people eat food that has been fried in oil, to remember the **miracle** of the oil in the **ner tamid**. Traditional fried foods such as potato latkes and doughnuts are popular.

Olive oil

The oil used in the **temple's** ever-burning light was olive oil. Olive trees grow well in the hot, dry climate of Israel, and some live to be thousands of years old. The olives are harvested and crushed to give their oil. Olive oil is delicious in dressings or used for cooking.

It is traditional to eat potato latkes at Hanukkah.

Making potato latkes

This recipe makes about 10 latkes. Ask an adult to help you.

You will need:

2 large potatoes
2 tablespoons plain flour
2 eggs
salt and pepper
oil for frying
a potato peeler, grater,
mixing bowl, frying pan
and fish slice

1. Peel and grate the potatoes, and drain away any liquid.
2. Beat the eggs and add a little salt and pepper.
3. Mix the potato and flour with the eggs.
4. Ask an adult to help you heat the oil in a frying pan.
5. Drop spoonfuls of the mixture into the pan, and flatten them a little with the spoon.
6. Fry for a few minutes until brown, then turn over and brown the other side.
7. Drain on kitchen paper, then serve straight away.

Playing the dreidle

It's fun to play the dreidle, a traditional game at Hanukkah. The **Hebrew** letters on each side of the dreidle stand for the words Nes Gadol Hayah Sham, which mean 'A great **miracle** happened there'.

How to play:
Everyone starts with six counters. First, everyone puts three counters in the pool. Then, each person takes a turn to spin the dreidle and do what it says. The winner is the person who gets all the counters.

If the dreidle lands showing the letter:

נ   Nun 'n', you do **n**othing

ג   Gimmel 'g', you **g**et everything in the pool

      Hey 'h', you take **h**alf of the pool (half plus one if there is an odd number)

      Shin 'sh', you '**sh**ell out' another counter into the pool.

How to make a dreidle

You will need: a piece of thin card, crayons, a drawing pin, scissors, ruler, glue, a small pencil, Plasticine

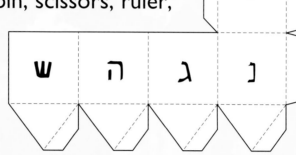

1. Draw and enlarge this shape onto thin card. Cut it out.
2. Write the Hebrew letters on each side.
3. Carefully make a tiny hole with a drawing pin at the centre of the top square.
4. Carefully score and fold along the dotted lines.
5. Stick the side tab in place to make the cube.
6. To make the point of the dreidle, glue and press the tabs into place using the point of a pencil.
7. When the glue is dry, press a blob of Plasticine into the point inside the base.
8. Stick the tabs at the top of the dreidle.
9. When the glue is dry, carefully press the pencil through the pinhole and into the Plasticine.

Around the world

In Israel, in the village of Modi'in where Mattathias lived, a great bonfire is held. Torches of freedom are carried by runners from there to all parts of the country, and even by plane to other countries, too.

On the seventh day of Hanukkah in Tunis, in north Africa, women would remember the day that Judith killed Holofernes. At the **synagogue** they would file past and kiss the Torah scroll.

Hanukkah celebrations in modern-day Israel. The shape of a hanukiah is lit up on a block of flats.

During the Second World War, a young Jewish girl called Anne Frank lived in hiding with her family while the Nazi armies occupied Holland. She wrote in her diary, 'We didn't make much fuss about Hanukkah: we just gave each other a few little presents and then we had the candles. Because of the shortage of candles we only had them alight for ten minutes.'

Anne Frank, who wrote a diary whilst hiding from the Nazis.

Religion was banned in Russia during communist rule. Many Russian Jews used to celebrate Hanukkah and other festivals secretly. If the police found out, Jews could lose their jobs or even be sent to prison. But since the early 1990s when the communist government fell, people of all religions have been able to **worship** freely there.

21

The Jewish calendar

The Jewish calendar is based on the moon. There are 12 months, each with 28 or 29 days. Each new month starts at the new moon.

Every few years an extra month, called Adar 2, is added to keep in step with the seasons. Here is the Jewish calendar showing some of the festivals.

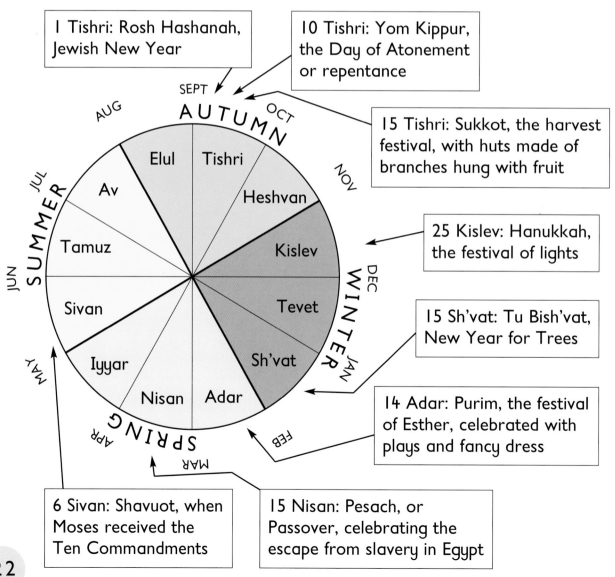

1 Tishri: Rosh Hashanah, Jewish New Year

10 Tishri: Yom Kippur, the Day of Atonement or repentance

15 Tishri: Sukkot, the harvest festival, with huts made of branches hung with fruit

25 Kislev: Hanukkah, the festival of lights

15 Sh'vat: Tu Bish'vat, New Year for Trees

14 Adar: Purim, the festival of Esther, celebrated with plays and fancy dress

6 Sivan: Shavuot, when Moses received the Ten Commandments

15 Nisan: Pesach, or Passover, celebrating the escape from slavery in Egypt

SEPT
AUG
OCT
AUTUMN
Elul Tishri
JUL
NOV
Av   Heshvan
SUMMER
Tamuz Kislev
JUN
Sivan Tevet
DEC
WINTER
Iyyar Sh'vat
JAN
MAY
Nisan Adar
SPRING
APR
MAR
FEB

Glossary

BCE Before the Common Era. People of all religions can use this, rather than the Christian BC, which counts from the birth of Jesus Christ. The year numbers are not changed.

Bible the Jews' holy book. Jews only use the first part of the Bible, sometimes called the Old Testament.

CE Common Era, the same as Christian AD. See BCE above.

hanukiah the eight-branched candlestick which is used at Hanukkah

Hebrew the language used by Jews for prayer. Hebrew is spoken by Jewish people in Israel.

holy respected because it is to do with God

idol a statue which is worshipped as a god

Judaism the religion followed by Jewish people

miracle something that God made happen

ner tamid the ever-burning light in a synagogue

rabbi a Jewish religious leader and teacher

religion belief in God or gods

Shabbat the Hebrew word for the sabbath, which for Jews is from Friday evening to Saturday evening

synagogue Jewish place of worship

temple a place of worship

worship to show respect and love for God

Index

Titles in the *Celebrations* series include:

Hardback   0 431 13796 X

Hardback   0 431 13790 0

Hardback   0 431 13793 5

Hardback   0 431 13791 9

Hardback   0 431 13794 3

Hardback   0 431 13795 1

Hardback   0 431 13792 7

Find out about the other titles in this series on our website www.heinemann.co.uk/library